Adventure with Alphabet

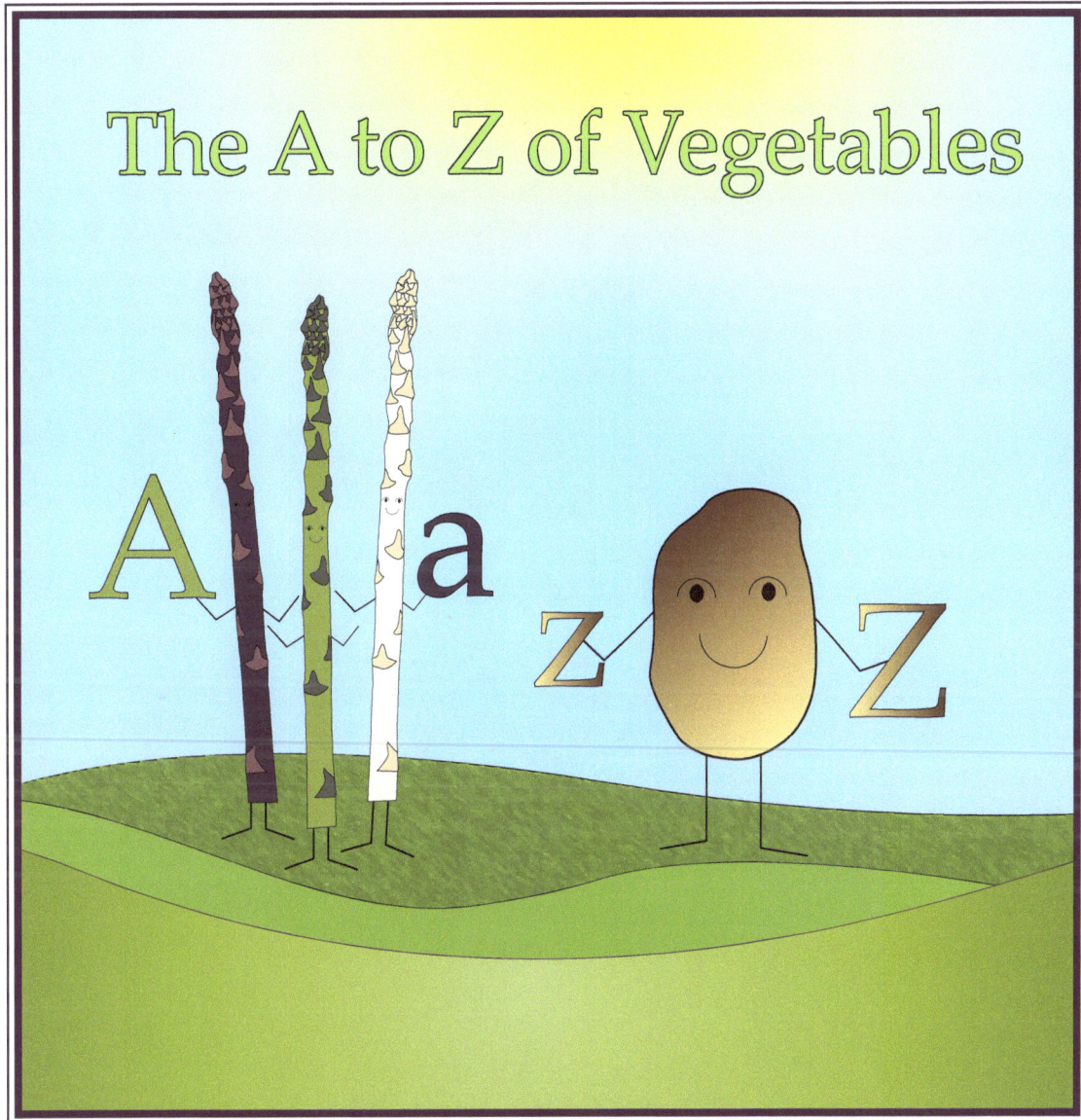

The A to Z of Vegetables

Written, Art & Design
by
Katarzyna Skrzyniecka & Mateusz Skrzyniecki

ISBN 979-8-88713-031-6
Library of Congress Control Number 2025911556

www.adventurewithalphabet.com

Adventure with Alphabet

The A to Z of Vegetables

THIS BOOK BELONGS TO

Aa Bb Cc Dd
Ee Ff Gg Hh Ii
Jj Kk Ll Mm
Nn Oo Pp Qq
Rr Ss Tt Uu Vv
Ww Xx Yy Zz

Curious Explorers!

Get ready for a tasty and vibrant journey through the alphabet!

From A to Z, each letter introduces a special vegetable,
bringing the garden to life in a fun and exciting way.

You'll meet some familiar favorites like
Carrot, Onion, and Ziemniak (Potato!),
but you'll also discover unique vegetables from around the world—
have you ever heard of Qaqoċċ, Ullucus, or Xi lanhua?

With each turn of the page, you'll explore new textures, colors,
and names while learning the alphabet one veggie at a time.

This book is a great way to build your knowledge, spark curiosity,
and celebrate the beauty of nature's harvest.

Whether you're reading alone or sharing with friends and family,
every page is a chance to learn something new.

So, let's begin our Alphabet Adventure—
what vegetable wonders will we find?

— Kasia & Mati

My English name is

Asparagus

My Italian name is Asparago.

Aa

My English name is
Beet
My Polish name is Burak.

Bb

My English name is
Carrot
My French name is Carotte.

C c

My English name is
Dandelion
My Spanish name is Diente de León.

Dd

My English name is

Endive

My Czech name is Endive.

E e

My English name is

Fennel

My Italian name is Finocchio.

Ff

My English name is
Garlic

My Polish name is Czosnek.

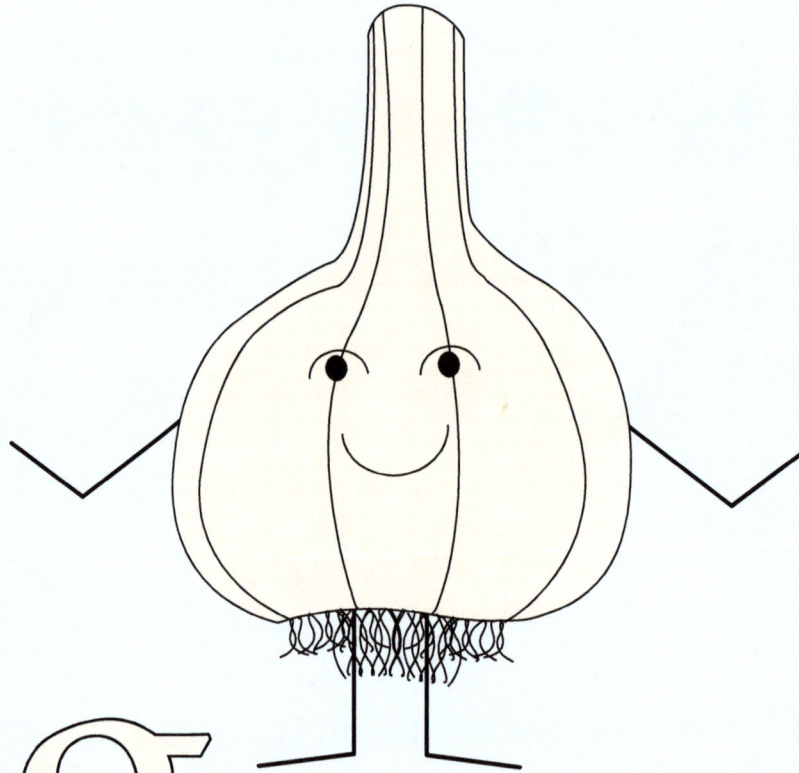

G g

My English name is
Horseradish
My French name is Raifort.

Hh

My English name is
Iceberg Lettuce
My Hungarian name is Jégsaláta.

Ii

My English name is

Jerusalem Artichoke

My Spanish name is Alcachofa de Jerusalén.

J j

My English name is
Kale
My Dutch name is Boerenkool.

K k

My English name is

Leek

My German name is Lauch.

My English name is
Mushroom
My Italian name is Fungo.

Mm

My English name is

Nasturtium

My Polish name is Nasturcja.

Nn

My English name is

Onion

My Spanish name is Cebolla.

Oo

My English name is

Parsnip

My German name is Pastinake.

P p

My Maltese name is
Qaqoċċ
My English name is Artichoke.

Q q

My English name is
Radish
My Czech name is Ředkev.

Rr

My English name is
Sorrel

My Polish name is Szczaw.

Ss

My English name is
Turnip
My Italian name is Rapa.

Tt

My English name is
Ulluco
My Hungarian name is Ullucus.

Uu

My Spanish name is
Vainita
My English name is Green Beans.

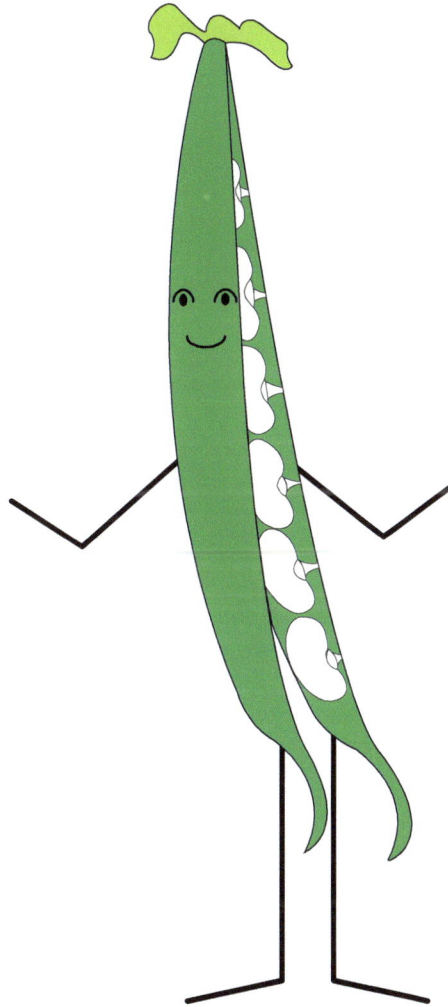

My English name is
Wild Leek
My Czech name is Divoký Pórek.

W w

My Chinese name is

Xī lán huā

My English name is Brocolli.

My English name is

Yam

My German name is Yamswurzel.

Yy

My Polish name is
Ziemniak
My English name is Potato.

Zz

Congratulations, Curious Explorers!

You've traveled from A to Z,
discovering vegetables from near and far—
tasting the alphabet, learning names,
and seeing how special each vegetable is!

Now that you've met all these colorful characters,
you might spot them at the market, on your dinner plate,
or even growing in a garden nearby.

Remember, every vegetable has its own story, flavor,
and secret to share—just like you!
Keep asking questions, trying new things,
and celebrating the wonders of the natural world.

Our veggie adventure may be over for now,
but your curiosity can keep growing every day.

Until our next crunchy, leafy, tasty tale…

Stay curious, stay rooted,
Kasia & Mati

www.ingramcontent.com/pod-product-compliance
Lightning Source LLC
LaVergne TN
LVHW072056070426
835508LV00002B/120